Know About Sardar Vallabhbhai Patel

MAPLE KIDS

KNOW ABOUT SARDAR VALLABHBHAI PATEL

ALL RIGHTS RESERVED. No part of this book may be reproduced in a retrieval system or transmitted in any form or by any means electronics, mechanical, photocopying, recording and or without permission of the publisher.

Published by

MAPLE PRESS PRIVATE LIMITED
office: A-63, Sector 58, Noida 201301, U.P., India
phone: +91 120 455 3581, 455 3583
email: info@maplepress.co.in
website: www.maplepress.co.in
Go to www.maplelibrary.com for more e-books.

Reprinted in 2019

ISBN: 978-93-50334-12-6

Contents

Preface 4
1. Vallabhbhai Patel - A Study... 5
2. Birth of a Legend 9
3. First School... 12
4. Short Tales on Patel 15
5. The Ambitious Lawyer... 19
6. The Telegram 23
7. The Coming of Gandhi.. 26
8. The Fearless Leader 29
9. The Perfect Organiser 32
10. The Hero of Bardoli 35
11. From Patel to Sardar Patel.. 39
12. Sharing Responsibilities 42
13. The Father of Unity 45
14. The Iron Man 48
15. Death of Gandhi... 52
16. Death of Sardar Patel 55
17. The Real Satyagrahi... 58
18. Patel's Tradition 61
19. The Able Middleman 64
20. Patel and Nehru 68
21. A Letter 71
22. Patel - The Man.. 74
23. Remembering Sardar Patel... 78

Preface

Sardar Vallabhbhai Patel, regarded as the founding father of the Republic of India, is famously known as the "Iron Man of India". With a commendable spirit of determination and dedication for his country, he was certainly one of the greatest leaders the country has ever witnessed.

Along with playing a vital role in India's struggle for freedom, he significantly contributed in the integration of the princely states to rebuild a united and independent India. If Gandhi inspired the masses towards independence, it was Patel who organized them into a fighting force.

After independence, he was appointed as the Deputy Prime Minister of India. He showed exemplary excellence in managing complex affairs of the state and constantly worked towards restoring peace in the country. As a token of respect, world's tallest statue, *The Statue of Unity*, was dedicated to him on 31 October 2018.

This book deals with the life and times of Sardar Patel whose actions and deeds reflected honesty and conviction, earning him the epithet of being a hero among heroes of modern India.

Chapter 1
Vallabhbhai Patel - A Study

Sardar Vallabhbhai Patel was born in Gujarat on 31 October 1875. He was the son of Laad Bai and Jhaverbhai Patel, who had served in the army of the Queen of Jhansi. Vallabhbhai started his education in a Gujarati medium school and pursued in English medium when he shifted to Nadiad High School after middle school. He successfully organized many events. He completed his matriculation in 1897.

In 1891, he married Jhaverbaben Patel. The couple had two children. Unfortunately, she passed away in 1909. In 1910, he went to England to study law. He returned back to India and started practicing law after completing his studies in 1913. He joined the Gujarat club and adopted a western lifestyle. One day, Gandhi arrived at the club to deliver a few lectures. His talks greatly influenced Patel. He rejected foreign clothes after his encounter with Gandhi. He diligently followed the rules of Satyagraha. A relationship of teacher and student began to develop between them.

In 1918, during the floods in Kaira, the British started collecting taxes from the farmers. Implementing the principles of Satyagraha, Patel asked the farmers to stop paying tax to the government. Following his advice, the farmers peacefully revolted against the tax-system. The British gave up and returned the lands back to the farmers. In 1928, the farmers faced a similar problem and Vallabhbhai came to their rescue again. The British had again imposed an unjust taxation, but the farmers of Bardoli, under the guidance of Vallabhbhai stayed strong. The government captured their lands. This continued for more than six months until Patel's brother Vithalbhai, an important figure in the Central Legislative Assembly, ended this in a peaceful manner.

This incident delighted Gandhi and he entitled him as *'Sardar'*. When Patel assisted Gandhi in

THE IRON MAN OF INDIA

the Salt Satyagraha, he faced imprisonment for the first time. He played a vital role in the formation of the Indian Union. With great wisdom and political knowledge, he united the small kingdoms and tackled the Nizam of Hyderabad and the Nawab of Junagarh, who at the beginning did not want to join India. India faced a lot of problems while the states decided whether to merge with India or Pakistan. Sardar Patel's effort towards uniting the whole country is unforgettable. Due to his contribution in the union, Sardar Patel was entitled as the 'Iron Man'. He was one of the respectable leaders of the world and will always be remembered for his struggle in uniting a divided nation without a tinge of bloodshed.

When India became free and Pakistan attacked Kashmir, Patel refused to return the cash left by the British for Pakistan. Gandhi found it immoral and fasted until death. Sardar withdrew his argument because he could not make his *Guru* undergo such suffering.

In independent India, he held several offices as the Home Minister, the Minister of State and the Minister for Information and Broadcasting.

One of his major achievements was the merger of the royal states into the Indian Union.

Chapter 2
Birth of a Legend

Sardar Vallabhbhai Patel, popularly known as the 'Man of Steel', was born at Nadiad in Gujarat on 31st October 1875. His father was Jhaverbhai Patel and his mother Laad Bai. Jhaverbhai was a poor farmer, yet strong in his belief and conviction. His country and freedom were as dear to him as his own life. In 1857, during the first struggle for India's freedom, Jhaverbhai fought bravely against the British.

Vithalbhai, Vallabhbhai's elder brother, was also a well-known patriot. He was the Chairman of the Indian Legislative Council.

During his early years, Vallabhbhai suffered from a boil in the armpit. He went to a man who was known to cure boils using hot iron. The man heated the iron rod till it grew red. But his treatment was getting delayed for some reason or the other.

Frustrated by such delay, he picked up the glowing rod and burnt the boil without a hint of pain on his face.

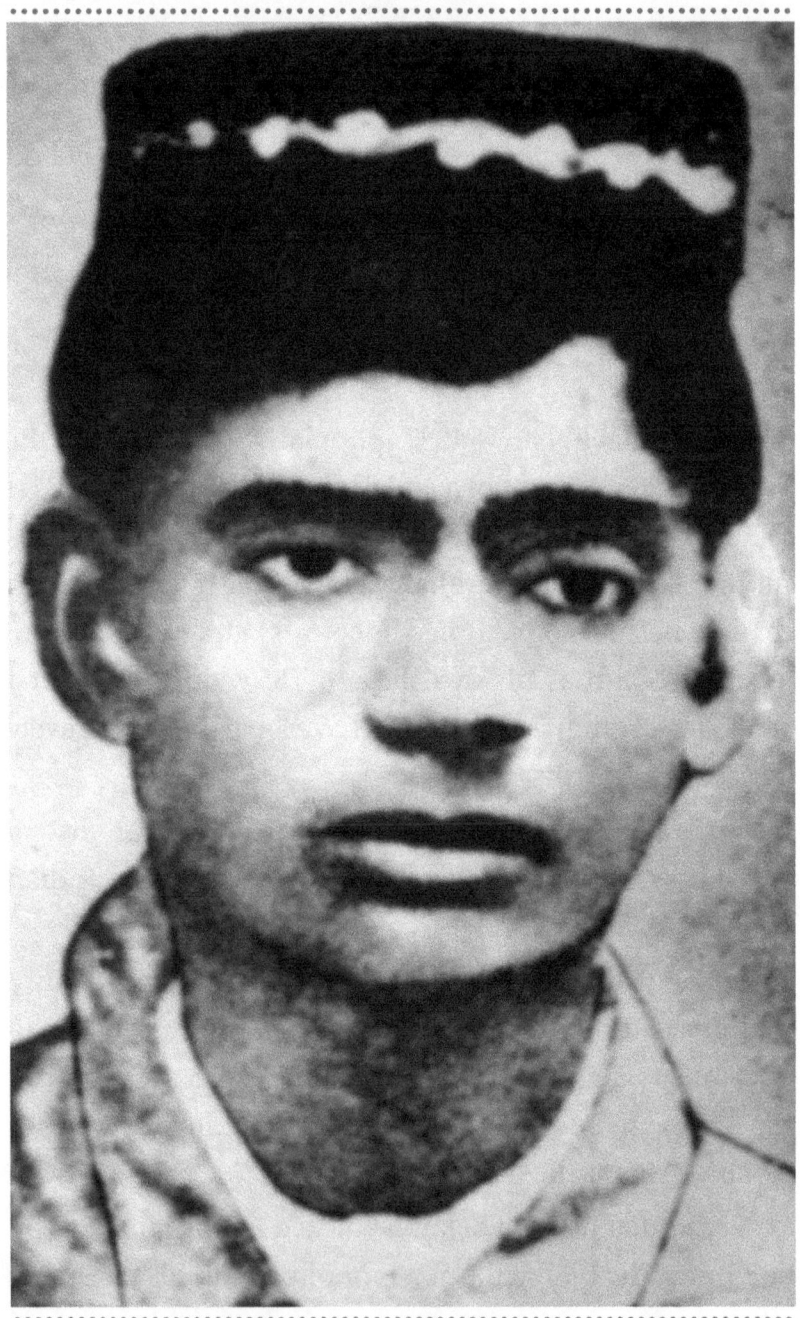

Witnessing such fearlessness, the onlookers were surprised and the younger ones stared in awe at him. He always stood against injustice. Though he belonged to a poor farmer family, he showed interest in the welfare of his companions, helping them in the best way he could. He always promoted friendship and unity.

Chapter 3
First School

Vallabh got the first lessons of education from his father. While other children were on the field, he was busy learning simple arithmetic and multiplication tables from his father. His character was moulded by both his parents who promoted the values of honesty, truthfulness and fearlessness. Vallabhbhai's pursued his early education in Karamsad and Petlad and completed his high school in Nadiad.

One of his teachers sold books as per the requirement of the pupils. But he used to force all the pupils to buy books from him and if any one disobeyed, the teacher would scold and punish him. Vallabhbhai did not support this. He spoke to his companions and made sure that not a single pupil attended his classes. For a whole week the school could not work due to this mass bunking and at last the teacher realized and rectified his actions.

When he was in Petlad, he cooked for himself. Every week he used to carry things from home and walk to Petlad as he had no money to buy train tickets for himself.

One fine day at school, a teacher made a mistake while working out a sum. Vallabhbhai pointed out the error. The teacher was angry and said, "All right, you be the teacher." The boy replied, "Very well, sir." He solved the sum correctly, and sat down in the teacher's chair!

Another incident which revealed the fearless nature of Vallabhbhai Patel is when he chose Gujarati over Sanskrit as his optional subject. The teacher, who taught Gujarati, liked Sanskrit more than his own subject. When Vallabhbhai entered his class, the teacher insulted him by addressing him as "great man!" He asked the boy, in anger, "Why did you give up Sanskrit and chose Gujarati?"

Vallabhbhai answered, "If everyone chose Sanskrit, you won't have any work."

This angered the teacher, who later complained to the headmaster. Vallabhbhai narrated the whole incident to the headmaster. The headmaster lauded him and said, "I have never seen such a brave student." This vexed the teacher. After that incident, Vallabhbhai left that school. He studied at home and successfully passed the examination.

Chapter 4
Short Tales on Patel

Vallabhbhai Patel was both precocious and fearless. One day at school, out of curiosity he asked his teacher, "Sir, why does the moon look smaller on some nights?" Hearing this, the teacher scolded him and shouted, "Stupid fool, how dare you open your mouth? Why do you ask me? Learn for yourself!" This reaction highly discouraged him and he promised himself that he would find the answers to the questions that would arise in his mind.

Such incidents in his early life, reflected the qualities of leadership and determination in him.

Vallabh attended a village school where there was a teacher who was extremely strict and short-tempered. Once he fined a student and turned him out of the class. As the student was poor and could not pay the fine, the boys thought the action to be unjust. Under Vallabh's leadership, they went on a strike. The strike was successful. After three days, the headmaster apologized on behalf of the teacher. He assured Vallabh and other students that none would be punished unjustly.

There was another incident, which took place during this period. One day, Vallabhbhai and his classmates were waiting for a teacher who always came late to class.

Almost fifteen minutes had passed but there was no sign of his arrival. Bored, one of the students began singing a song and later the whole class gave him company. The sounds of chorus, clapping of hands and desks filled the whole atmosphere with a lot of noise. Suddenly, the door opened and the teacher entered into the class.

"How dare you make such a noise!" shouted the teacher. The whole class became silent. There was pin-drop silence. In the meantime, Vallabh stood up and said calmly, "Sir, we were waiting for you and as you were late and we had nothing else to do, we decided to entertain ourselves."

The teacher couldn't control his anger and shouted, "You naughty boy! Have you come to the school to sing?"

Vallabh replied fearlessly, but humbly, "No, it is not

that, sir. We are here to get education. But as there was no teacher in our class, we decided to sing. Were we wrong?"

"Get out of the class!" replied the teacher angrily.

Obeying the teacher's orders, he took up his books and left the class. But, the teacher pulled him to the headmaster's office and complained about the happenings. Hearing which, the headmaster scolded him, "You should respect your teachers and should not answer back. Say sorry at once!"

But Vallabh replied calmly, "Sir, with due respect, do you support a teacher coming late to class? Mr. Aggarwal always comes late to our class. He wastes our precious time too."

The headmaster enquired about it and asked the teacher to attend the classes on time. Vallabh was sent back to the class. The teacher was never late again.

These incidents, undoubtedly, signify the making of the 'Iron Man'.

Chapter 5
The Ambitious Lawyer

Vallabhbhai's primary aim was to become a lawyer. In order to fulfill this, he needed to pursue his studies in England. But, his family was too poor to afford such an expense.

In those days, a candidate could study in private and sit for the law examination. Vallabhbhai's brother, Vithalbhai, was also a lawyer. He had attended coaching classes before sitting for the examination. But, Vallabhbhai did not even attend such classes. Instead he borrowed books from a lawyer who was his friend and studied their judgments. He occasionally attended courts. He listened attentively to the lawyers' arguments. He observed all types of lawyers -the frightened, the bold and the skillful ones. And finally, Vallabhbhai passed the law examination.

Vallabhbhai had no provisions to begin his practice of law. He borrowed some money and hired a room in a town called Godhra. He furnished it with a couple of chairs and mats for those who wished to sit on the floor.

His vibrant personality soon attracted clients. Whichever subject he chose, Vallabhbhai made a thorough study of it.

Gradually, Vallabhbhai became a very famous lawyer. By then, he was married to Jhaverba. The couple had two children, a daughter, Manibehn and a son, Dahyabhai Patel.

Meanwhile, Vallabhbhai's wife fell ill and was sent to Bombay for her treatment. In 1908, she was operated for the removal of a harmful tumour.

Sardar Vallabhbhai Patel wished to become a lawyer. He was saving money to go to England to pursue his studies in law. He wrote a letter to a travel agency about his trip to England. He eagerly waited for the envelope with the ticket to arrive. But destiny had some other plans.

One afternoon, Vallabh's elder brother, Vithal came rushing to him happily and said, "See what luck has come my way! Some unknown friend has sent me a ticket to England, together with a passport!" Vallabh was happy to see the envelope and snatched it from his brother and exclaimed, "This is my ticket, not yours!"

Both of them glanced at the address written on the envelope. It was neatly and correctly written, *Mr. V.J Patel,*

Pleader, Borsad. Vallabh realized how the letter reached Vithal.

When Vallabh told everything to Vithal, he was sad. But, being elder to Vallabh, Vithal pleaded, "I am elder to you. Let me go to England. After I return, you will get a chance to go too."

Vallabh felt opportunities slipping from his hands. But, how could he refuse his brother? At last he agreed, "All right. You can take these papers and set sail for England. After all, they are in your name! And if you need money in England write to me. I shall send you the money."

At last, Vithalbhai boarded the ship to England. The action by the younger brother won the love and respect of everybody who came to know about the incident. Vithalbhai was lucky to have a selfless brother as Vallabhbhai Patel.

Chapter 6
The Telegram

One day, Vallabhbhai had an important case. He was diligently arguing for his case before the judge. In the midst of events, an urgent telegram was handed to him. Undisturbed, he read the letter, put it in his pocket and went on with the argument. It was only after ending his speech that he sat down. Everyone in the court knew that the telegram announced the death of his wife.

Vallabhbhai had such sense of duty that even the news of his wife's death could not break his dedication! Troubles never discouraged him. With an amour of strong willpower, he effectively completed whichever task he undertook.

Patel was only thirty-three years old when his wife died. He never remarried.

After his brother's return, Vallabhbhai went to England. He solely focused on his studies. Even the glitter and luxury of the fashionable life of England could not tempt him. The library was at a distance of eleven miles

from his place. Every morning he walked to the library. After intense labor and hard work, he stood first in the Barrister-at-Law Examination.

As soon as he returned to India, Vallabhbhai set up practice as a senior lawyer at Ahmedabad. During this time his elder brother, Vithalbhai, said, "You look after the family; I shall work for the country". Vallabhbhai willingly agreed.

At that time, Vallabh was earning eight to ten thousand rupees a month. He spent his leisure playing cards in a local club. He dressed like the English. Politics did not interest him and he sometimes joked at the idea of dedicating one's life for the country as pointless dreams of crazy fellows.

Chapter 7
The Coming of Gandhi

Gradually, the spell of Gandhi spread all over Gujarat. It touched Vallabhbhai's life too. Gandhi attended the Political Conference at Godhra. Gandhi had a number of followers and admirers. Vallabhbhai also knew about Gandhi and soon got acquainted with him and became friends.

Patel was very fond of children, but he failed to show any affection. When Manibehn would shyly ask him, "How

are you, father?" he would answer as briefly as possible, "I'm all right."

Dahyabhai also tried to talk to his father but Vallabhbhai never responded.

The training Manibehn received cultivated many good qualities in her. She was instilled with the values, good habits and eternal love for simple living. When public life pressurized her father, she devoted herself to his service. She became his private secretary, took care of his health and found joy and fulfillment in serving him. She was sure that she could best serve the country by sharing his burden.

Patel -A friend of the farmers

In 1918, heavy rains destroyed the crops in Gujarat. The farmers in Kaira District were in distress. The Government demanded the payment of the taxes. The farmers turned to Gandhi for help.

Gandhi said, "I need someone who will take the whole responsibility for this struggle."

"I shall be responsible," said Vallabhbhai Patel and took the leadership of the struggle. He encouraged the farmers to muster courage to revolt against the British by staying united.

Vallabhbhai gave up his western clothes and dressed as a simple farmer. He walked from village to village and promoted unity among the farmers. The farmers were filled with love and respect. He struggled for them day and night. The farmers did as directed and were ready to dedicate their lives to him. Finally, the government yielded and the taxes were cancelled. Thus, the struggle led by Patel was successful. In June 1918, the farmers celebrated their victory. They invited Gandhi. In his speech, Gandhi said, "The credit of this victory should go to Vallabhbhai Patel. You are fortunate to be led, by such a great hero."

Patel replied with modesty, "The people of Kaira district have fought with courage and energy. The honour of this success goes to them."

Chapter 8
The Fearless Leader

Vallabhbhai lived up to his ideals. In 1920, the Congress Party passed a resolution on non-cooperation. The policy of non-cooperation resolved not to cooperate with the

foreign government in any way. Patel gave up his practice as a lawyer, which used to bring him thousands of rupees every month. He asked people not to send their children to schools run by the government. He founded the Gujarat Vidyapeeth to educate the children and mould them to grow up as patriots. He collected lakes of rupees for the building of this institution.

In 1923, the government banned the tricolor flag in the roads of Nagpur, where government officers lived. This severely angered the leaders and the people. Therefore, they decided to act against the order and invited Vallabhbhai Patel to guide them. As soon as he arrived, the struggle grew stronger and Satyagrahis began to pour in from other parts of the country. The fight went on for three and a half months. Finally, the government had to

withdraw the order and the Satyagraha ended in a victory of the people.

The people of Borsad *taluk* were subjected to great suffering at that time. A dacoit, Babar and his gang began a series of murders and lootings. A police force was enforced to put them down. But the police became as troublesome as the robbers. Instead of protecting, they frightened the people and took away money, jewels and grains. Meanwhile, the government imposed a new tax on the people to meet the expenses of the police force. This further insulted them. The people were unjustly burdened.

Vallabhbhai raced to rescue the people. He formed a team of young volunteers from the neighboring villages to protect against the bandits. As soon as these young men swung into action, the dacoits disappeared.

Patel firmly clarified to the Government, "We do not need your police force and we are not going to pay the new tax." The officers of the government tried to frighten the people in a number of ways. But their tricks were of no use. The government had to withdraw its order. Vallabhbhai's fame spread to every nook and corner of India.

Chapter 9
The Perfect Organiser

Patel grew more and more attracted to Gandhi once he got closely acquainted to him. It brought about a lot of changes in Patel's life. Patel stopped wearing European suits and began attiring himself in *khadi*, *kurtas* and *dhoti*. He even stopped going to the court. He started to believe in simple living, simple eating, doing one's own works like washing clothes and sweeping his room.

In the year 1923, Gujarat underwent massive destruction due to heavy rains. There were floods everywhere. The roads were under water. Thousands of houses were washed away. There were huge loss of life and people. Vallabhbhai came to their rescue. His efforts brought about 2,000 volunteers together. They supplied food and clothes to those who suffered due to the floods and also looked after them.

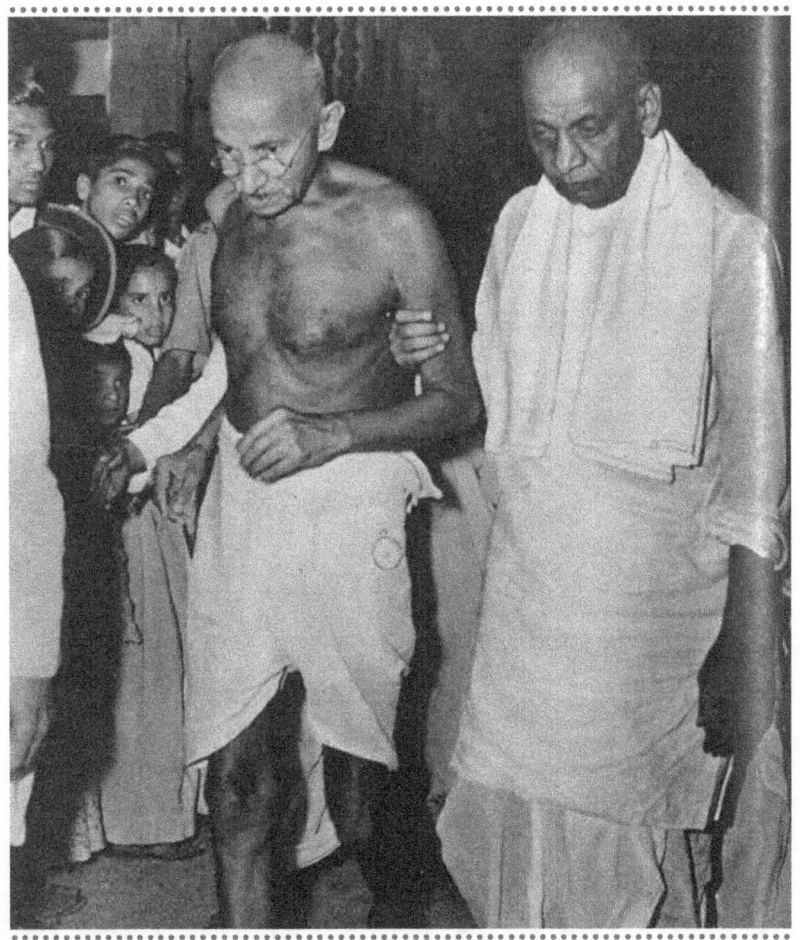

But their services were still not enough. The flood was followed by a terrible famine. The farmers had no oxen, and no seeds. During this hour, Patel came as the 'Messiah' to the people. He drew the attention of the government to the sufferings of the people. He argued that as the government collected taxes from the people, it was the duty of the government to help them in their times of trouble. Finally, the government was forced to spend fifteen million rupees to help those in the famine stricken areas. Patel organized the relief works properly, to make sure that the money was properly utilized. The world realized that he was not only a great fighter, but also a perfect organizer.

Chapter 10
The Hero of Bardoli

Bardoli is a *taluk* in Gujarat. The people of this *taluk* greatly suffered from floods and famines. To add on to their sufferings, the foreign government hiked the taxes by thirty percent. The people did not know what to do. They went to Vallabhbhai Patel and said, "You are our only hope."

Patel replied, "If you oppose the government, your sufferings will multiply. You will lose your lands and houses. The Government will do its best to break you. You will not have a grain of rice or a drop of milk and the women and the children will suffer in misery. Consider well. If you are confident that you have the courage to face all this, then let us fight."

"We are ready. We will rather die than bow down to injustice," said the farmers.

Patel wrote to the Governor and requested him to reduce the taxes. But, he did not react to Patel's letter instead the government announced the date of the collection of

the taxes. Patel strictly instructed the farmers not to pay any taxes. Patel divided Bardoli district into several zones. Each zone had a centre which was managed by a leader and some volunteers. Messengers were employed to carry messages from one centre to another. Patel also appointed spies to report on the movements of government officials.

"We shall use all our powers and break the struggle movement," declared the Governor of Bombay. The Government sent gangsters to frighten the villagers. The gangsters entered villages and violently harassed the villagers. They forcefully entered the houses and carried away grains, goods and money. They insulted the women. But, the farmers refused to give up. They did not pay a single pie.

The government began to sell the houses and lands. But, not a single man came forward to buy them. Vallabhbhai appointed volunteers in every village to keep a watch. As soon as he sighted the officials coming to sell the property, the volunteer would sound his bugle and the farmers would leave the village and hide in the jungles. Thus, the officials would find the whole village empty. They could never find the rightful owners of the houses and thus

failed to demarcate which house belonged to whom. Patel constantly encouraged and guided the villagers. He constantly assured the villagers that they have nothing to fear and the government had everything to lose.

"I, too, am a farmer," said Patel. "I know the mind of the farmers. I want that the farmers should be respected and be able to hold their heads erect. I can have peace of mind only when that is achieved."

Patel learnt that some rich men were coming from cities to buy the lands of the farmers, which were being sold. "I am the *Sardar*," declared Patel, "let them come, I know what to do." There was total social boycott of those who bought the lands. The rich men, who arrived could not get a grain of rice or a drop of water and immediately left the place.

Chapter 11
From Patel to Sardar Patel

By this time, several members of the Bombay Legislative Assembly opposed the unjust policies and resigned. The government lost and people's anger won. Vallabhbhai came to be known as Sardar Vallabhbhai Patel.

The farmers of Bardoli presented him with a formal speech and praised his greatness and leadership. In reply Patel said, "It was Mahatma Gandhi who gave me the herb of Satyagraha. All that I did was to administer the medicine. And you strictly followed that doctor's instructions. So, all that you have said in praise of me in your speech should belong to him and to you. The prosperity of the country is in the hands of the youth. Do not forget that in every country, it is the young who have won freedom and passed it on to later generations."

He was popularly known as the Sardar. But soon Sardar's words and actions angered the British government. It sent him to prison twice in 1930. But on the contrary, this further increased his fame. Sardar Patel was elected as the President of the Karachi Session of the National Congress,

which met in 1931. In his speech, Patel declared, "*Swaraj* or independence is our goal. No one can move away from that goal." This angered the government and he was imprisoned again. He was freed only in 1934.

Sardar's prison experiences are an interesting read. He was treated as an ordinary prisoner. There was only one washroom in the prison. Every morning the prisoners had to stand in line for their turn and had to wait in another line for water. There was no proper place for urination. The food was not properly served in the prison. But nothing could break the willpower of Sardar.

He befriended several other prisoners. Some of them gifted Sardar a few articles for his use in the prison. Amidst the gifts was a razor which the officials did not allow Patel to possess. Patel protested against it. He said, "Why are you not giving me the razor and let me shave all the prisoners? That will give me some work to do and I can spend my time."

Everyone, including the clerks who heard him, burst into laughter.

Patel's faith in God and religion was not openly known to all, but when he was in prison he got copies of the Bhagavad Gita and the Ramayana through the officials of the prison. He studied them every day.

Chapter 12
Sharing Responsibilities

The elections to the Legislatures of Provinces were held in 1937. Sardar was the Chairman of the Congress Parliamentary Board. Under his leadership, the Congress won a majority of seats in eight provinces and formed ministries. The offices of all of them were in the hands of the Sardar.

In 1942, the Congress called on the British to quit India. Thus, the 'Quit India Movement' or the *'Chale jav Movement'* took place.

During this time, Sardar Patel encountered the young leader who courageously hoisted the tricolor at river Ravi. He was Jawaharlal Nehru, whom Gandhi treated as his son, while he loved Patel as his younger brother.

The year when Motilal Nehru was to vacate the seat of the Congress presidentship Gandhi had to make a choice between Sardar Patel and Jawaharlal as his successor. But, Gandhi chose the younger man Jawaharlal Nehru as the successor. Patel accepted the decision with due respect. Even after independence, when Gandhi had to decide about the future India's Prime Minister, he voted for Nehru.

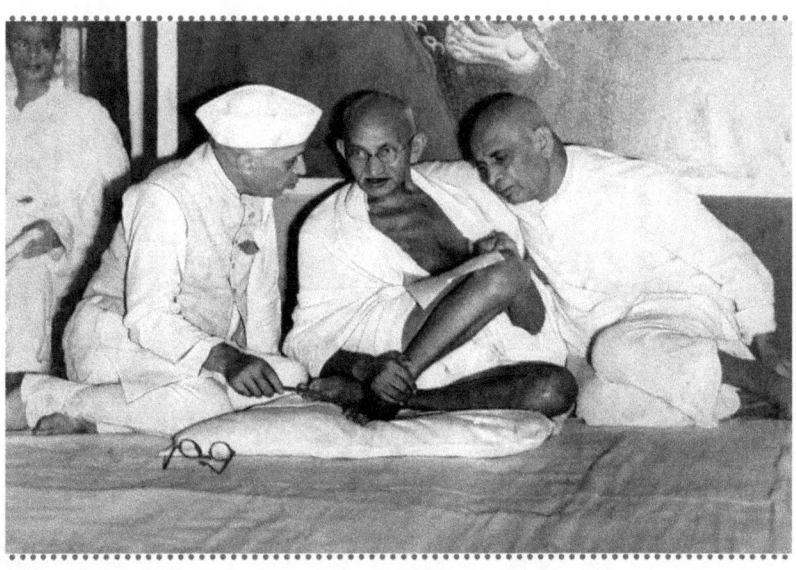

As a result of the 'Quit India Movement', the government jailed all the important leaders of the Congress, including Sardar Patel. Patel fell ill in the prison. He was not given proper medical assistance. The leaders were released after three years. At that time, the Muslim League created problems and hindered in the path of achieving freedom. Patel declared, "We shall fight all those who come in the way of India's freedom."

Finally, India got her freedom on 15 August 1947. Pandit Jawaharlal Nehru became the first Prime Minister of independent India. Sardar Patel became the Deputy Prime Minister. He was in charge of Home Affairs, Information and Broadcasting and the Ministry of States.

Chapter 13
The Father of Unity

There were more than 600 states in India at that time. Out of which only a few were small states. Some of the Maharajas and Nawabs, who ruled over these, were patriotic and wise. But, most of them were drunk in wealth and power. They dreamt of becoming independent rulers once the British quit India. They fought with the government of free India to treat them as equals. Some of them also planned to send their representatives to the United Nations Organization.

It was important to merge these states and make them a part of free India so as to avoid several problems that India would have likely faced. Otherwise, India might have had to take their regular permissions for the passage of trains through their states. If interstate rivers flowed through these states, India would have had to seek their permission to use the waters. Their permission would have been needed to build dams. And, in the event of a war between India and any other country, these 600

states would be confused about their existence. These 600 states would have been 600 sores on the body of India. The question of one of them, Kashmir, was not settled immediately. Even now Pakistan occupies a part of that state.

If the problem of the states were not solved quickly then there would have been several problems similar to that of Kashmir. "If we unite, we can soon make this country prosperous. Come and join us. Cooperate with us," said Sardar. He invited the rulers even before the Independence Day, but on one condition that they had to join before 15th of August, or else their position would be different. They would fail to get the respect and allowance they used to get before. Patel also met a number of rulers and held discussions with them. As a result, a number of patriotic rulers joined the Indian Union.

Chapter 14
The Iron Man

The rulers of Junagadh and Hyderabad were secretly planning to join Pakistan. Patel sent an army under Brigadier Guru dayal Simha to the border of Junagadh to deal with Pakistan. The people of the state, who wished to join India rose against the ruler and set up a People's Government. The Nawab, who tried to betray the people, ran away. Patel reached Junagadh on 12 November 1947. In the course of his speech, he warned that the Nizam of Hyderabad would face the situation that the Nawab of Junagadh faced if he did not behave wisely.

But the Nizam was slow to learn the lesson. He sent millions of rupees to Pakistan. One of his men, Kasim Razvi by name, began to harass the Hindus. His gang was called the *Razakars*. They tried to drive the Hindus out of Hyderabad. There was no limit to their crimes. They got arms and ammunitions from outside.

Finally, Sardar Patel sent some forces under General Chowdhury to undertake 'Police action'. Within five days,

the Nizam was forced to surrender. Kasim Razvi ran away to Pakistan. The problems created by the Razakars came to an end and peace returned to Hyderabad. The firm policy of Sardar Patel broke down all the plots against India.

A similar problem arose in Kashmir. The Maharaja and the Legislative Assembly decided that the state should join India. But, the Pakistan army forcefully occupied two-fifths of Kashmir. The Ministry handed over the Kashmir issue to be dealt by the Foreign Affairs.

Sardar Patel took decisions by keeping the future at sight. In 1962, China sent its army across the border and India was under its attack. This is the saddest episode in the history of free India. But, on 7 November 1950, Patel wrote a letter to Jawaharlal Nehru and warned that China

was not to be trusted. He wrote that, "The Government of China speaks of its desire for peace and then tries to mislead India. Hereafter, in planning the defenses of India, all ministers must remember the aims of Communist China."

Five weeks later Patel passed away. About twelve years after his death, China attacked India.

'I Must Speak the Truth'

Many people misunderstood Patel. A number of false rumors prevailed about his dislike towards Muslims. On 6 January 1948, speaking in Lucknow, he said, "There is a cry that I am against Muslims. But I am their true friend. I cannot beat about the bush. I cannot dissemble. Let no one try to have his two feet in two different boats. Let everyone choose one boat. Let us all, who belong to India, swim or sink together."

Though some of his words created controversy and agitation yet, his self-confidence was commendable. He stood by his conviction of speaking the truth and didn't break it just to please the audience.

Chapter 15
Death of Gandhi

Nathuram Godse, killed Gandhi on 30 January 1948. Gandhi was like an elder brother and *guru* to Patel. They had been put in the same jail several times. During their days in prison, Gandhi said, "Vallabhbhai's affection for me reminded me of my mother. Before this time I had not realized that such a loving and caring heart was hidden in him."

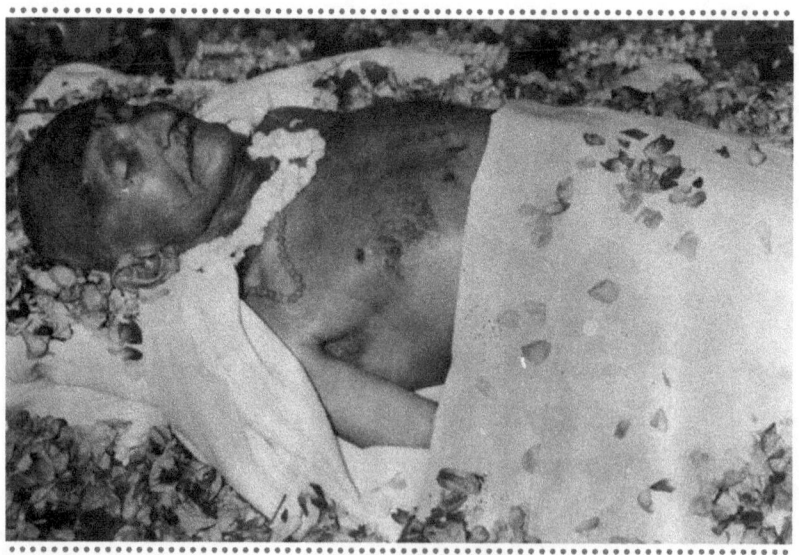

Patel was famously known as the 'Iron Man'. But beneath his strict composure, was a loving heart. He not only looked after Gandhi, but also other friends like Kania Lal Munshi with the affection of a mother, when they were in prison.

Patel was the last person to meet Gandhi before Mahatma was shot dead at the prayer meeting.

When the news of Gandhi's death reached him, Patel was reading the newspaper at his residence. Patel immediately rushed to Birla House and sat down on a marble seat. Nehru rushed a little later and wept like a child near Bapuji's body. It was Patel's task to console all the visitors. Gandhi's death shook Patel and he could not sleep for several nights. Gandhi's assassination brought both Nehru and Patel closer to each other and they began to work together to govern the country.

Sardar Patel undertook several measures to uphold the greatness of India. The sight of the great Somanatha Temple in ruins because of the repeated attacks of foreigners pricked his heart. He undertook measures in rebuilding that temple. He made it the symbol of the power and victory of rising India, who had freed itself from slavery of centuries and felt a new energy running in its veins. It was from him that Kania Lal Munshi got the idea and founded the *Bharatiya Vidya Bhavan* in Bombay.

Chapter 16
Death of Sardar Patel

Once, the flight on which Patel was travelling, had to make a forced landing on the bank of a river, at a distance of about thirty miles from Jaipur as the engine of the plane failed. The Delhi airport lost all contact with the airplane. For about four hours they had no clue as to what had happened. But luckily, Sardar was safe.

Two days later, Sardar entered the Lok Sabha. Forgetting all rules, the members greeted him with *Sardar Patel Jindabad*.

The Speaker congratulated Sardar who was unhurt and said, "The misery and the anxiety of the entire nation until news came that he was safe shows what place he has won in the hearts of the people."

Eight days later, the members of Parliament held a function to felicitate him.

Even in his old age, Sardar was so busy that he did not have a moment's rest. He toured all over the country and this adversely affected his health. He passed away in

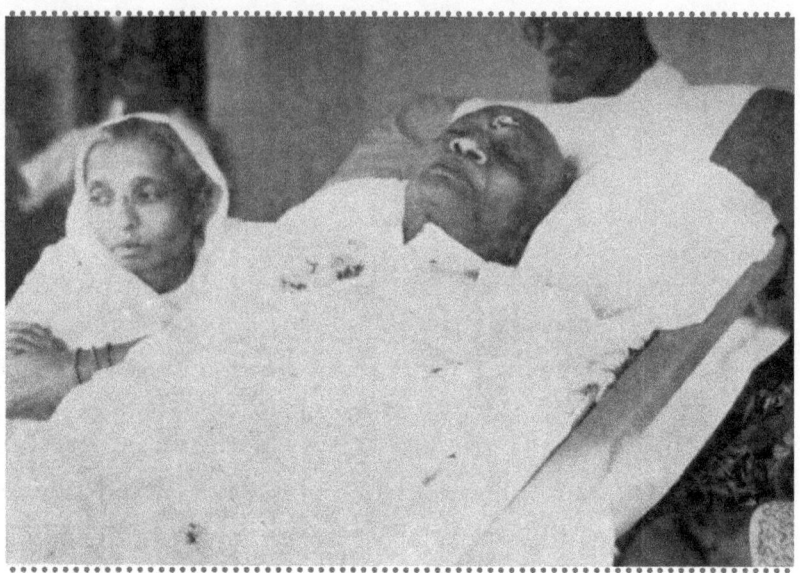

Bombay on the morning of the 15 December 1950. The General of Bardoli, the Lion of Gujarat, India's Man of Iron, the Sardar of the country's fight for freedom, the mighty former of the Union of India, Vallabhbhai Patel of rock-like will power, was no more.

Patel left no property. He had made no provision for his daughter. He didn't have a watch and his spectacles were 30 years old with strings.

Prime Minister Nehru said, "His name will live forever in history. He was the Maker of Modern India. He was a wise counselor in the hour of trial, a trustworthy friend and a mine of courage and influence."

Sardar Vallabhbhai Patel did not believe in making speeches. He was a man of few words. He calmly accepted both happiness and sorrows. He was very cordial and friendly. After the Bardoli Satyagraha, he became famous all over India. When he went to attend the Congress Session, he forgot to take his pass with him. The volunteers stopped him. So, he went back. Next day when the volunteers came to know who he was, they were ashamed. But Patel was not at all displeased.

It has been hundred years since the Sardar, was born, but even today he is remembered with respect and children are taught to follow his qualities at school.

Chapter 17
The Real Satyagrahi

One day, Sardar Patel was walking in his garden at his residence at Aurangzeb Road in Delhi. Suddenly, he was conveyed a message that sailors of the Royal Indian Navy had revolted and they were on the streets of Bombay. Although their demand was to increase their salaries, still the revolt turned into an anti-British riot. Anybody who tried to oppose them was attacked with bullets. Three

thousand sailors drove all over the city in vehicles with Congress and League flags. Patel quickly headed towards Bombay. He saw burnt-down buildings, looted shops and streets littered with stones, sticks and bottles. He decided to meet these mutineers.

As he reached to the spot, one of the sailors said, "We do not want to serve the British and therefore we like to overthrow the British from the Indian soil. We have faith in you and we want you to take over the Navy."

Patel smiled and replied, "My friend, our method of struggle was never to adopt any violent means to oppose anybody. These actions would convince the British that Indians will never be fit to govern themselves."

The sailors were shocked at the reply. They felt guilty about their acts. Patel added, "It is my humble request to

all of you to put down your arms and I assure you that no action will be taken against you." The sailors sincerely obeyed his words and one by one, all of them laid down their arms in front of the Sardar. Their leader said, "We are not surrendering to the British, but to our own people."

Nehru showered upon Patel words of praise and remarked, "I have not struggled for twenty-eight years to hand-over India to mutineers and violent men."

The incident proved Sardar Vallabhbhai as a true Satyagrahi and a ardent follower of Gandhian principles.

Chapter 18
Patel's Tradition

A notable biography of Rajmohan Gandhi contributes a lot to Sardar Vallabhbhai Patel and to the freedom of India and his significant role in the post-Independence period and also about his deeds and acts that has been forgotten.

It is commendable that P. N. Chopra and Prabha Chopra, eminent historians and authors of several

historical works, have now edited Manibehn Patel's diary, 1936-35, published by Vision Books, New Delhi. Earlier, P.N. Chopra had edited 15 volumes of Vallabhbhai Patel's correspondence and other material connected with his activities. The diary, unpublished and originally written in Gujarati which is now translated into English, covers the period from 8 June 1936 to 15 December 1950. Manibehn Patel's diary tells the inside story of the Congress which was torn by ideological conflicts and personal enmity among the top-ranking leaders, who were fighting against each other and thereby threatening national interests. It was Gandhi who by his powerful influence and skills resolved those issues.

In 1936, there was a crisis in the Congress Party when Nehru, as the Congress President, jealously attacked the princely states and the zamindari system. Patel, Rajendra Prasad, G. B. Pant, C. Rajagopalachari and Bhula Bhai Desai thought that Nehru's campaign against these powerful elements would be injurious to their interests in the forthcoming elections. They resigned in protest from the Congress Working Committee. Ultimately, Gandhi had to finish up these differences.

The diary discloses that in 1940, once again, the Congress leadership was divided. Gandhi was completely left alone, while other leaders such as Patel, Nehru and Sarojini Naidu were ready to willingly support the British war effort if the British provided India the right to self-government. Gandhi was uncompromising on the principle of non-violence and was determined to keep the country out of the war. Any participation in the war violated his commitment to the principle of non-violence. The diary reveals that Gandhi's threat to fast unto death at this time compelled the Congress to accept his leadership. The Congress, therefore, refused to help the British war effort.

Chapter 19
The Able Middleman

Manibehn's diary reveals Patel as an able middleman. It discloses for the first time that at the meeting of the Congress Working Committee held at Wardha on July 13, 1942, Gandhi was annoyed with the Congress President Maulana Azad due to political differences with him. He compelled Maulana to resign from the presidential office. This was just before launching the Quit India Movement.

At this critical time, Patel helped wisely to tide over the crisis. During the period from 1936-42, Gandhi dictated Congress policies. He gained power and any leader who opposed his policies, even a loyal man like Subhas Chandra Bose, was expelled from the Congress. Thus, Bose left the country in order to start his battle against the British in Europe and Southeast Asia.

There are certain gaps in the diary, from 31 August 1939 to 9 January 1940 and from 9 August 1942 to 13 June 1945. The former gap was when the Congress leaders were thrown into prison due to individual Satyagraha Movement and the latter gap was due to the Quit India Movement.

The diary records that the Congress President Azad was directing a settlement with the Cabinet Mission in 1946, without the knowledge of his colleagues in the Congress Working Committee. This angered Gandhi. For this conduct, Azad was forced to make way for Nehru as the Congress President. Later, Gandhi was to oppose even Azad's appointment as the Education Minister in the Interim Government.

The diary also records that V.P. Menon, the Constitutional Advisor to the British Government, shared close relations with Patel in early 1947. He kept him informed about the British policies on political matters. Menon was Patel's devoted follower. Patel was not the man to miss any opportunity. He regarded politics as a

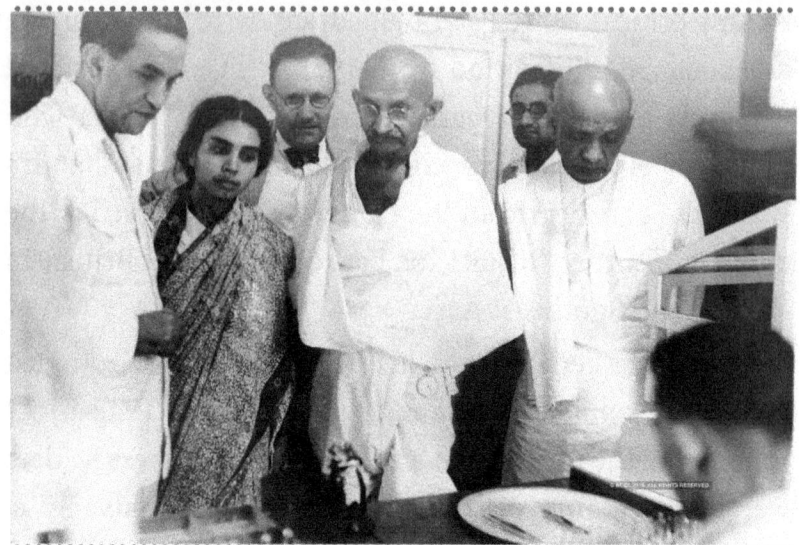

game of chess to be played using skill. Despite Gandhi's opposition, Patel accepted the Cabinet Mission statement of 16 May 1946, which permitted the Congress to join the Viceroy Lord Wavell's Executive Council and get power within the framework of the 1935 Constitution. This move by Patel served as a barrier for Jinnah's aim of keeping the Congress out of power.

There is also a detailed record of Patel breaking Jinnah's aim of merging Punjab and Bengal into Pakistan. Jinnah launched his Direct Action Movement to overthrow Punjab and North Western Frontier Province ministries. Bengal was already ruled by the Muslim League under the controlling authority of Jinnah.

Against Gandhi's wishes, again, the Congress Working Committee on 8 March 1947 passed a resolution for the

Partition of Punjab. It is clear from the diary that Patel had made a deal with Lord Mountbatten to transfer the power to India as soon as possible with Mountbatten as its Governor-General. The British Cabinet in England agreed to this plan. Thus, by saving the parts of Punjab and Bengal, Patel showed his highest qualities of statesmanship.

Chapter 20
Patel and Nehru

As already mentioned in the previous chapters, Gandhi's death brought two great leaders close to each other. But, this ended shortly due to fundamental differences that existed between them on basis of their ways to lead the country. Both of them were great men by all standards. But the issue of Hyderabad created a crack between Nehru and Patel. The Nizam of Hyderabad was determined to keep

his state independent and he was supported by Jinnah, the Governor-General of Pakistan. C. Rajagopalchari, the Governor-General of India, and Nehru wanted to lead military action on Hyderabad. But Patel thought otherwise. The Nizam took the Hyderabad issue to the United Nations. Patel remarked that, the Nizam does not think about his state and its problems. Thus, Patel worked his way and successfully merged Hyderabad into India. He ensured that unity prevailed in India.

Towards the end of 1948, Patel was unhappy with Nehru's way of tackling the national issues of the country. He also felt that he no longer enjoyed Nehru's confidence. He wrote to Nehru that no self-respecting man could work with him in the cabinet. He was convinced that Nehru was misguided on the Kashmir policy by N. Gopalaswami Ayyanger and Sheikh Abdullah. He told Bakshi Ghulam

Mohammad on 8 April 1948 that if he were given a free hand as in Hyderabad, he would solve the Kashmir problem in no time. He also disliked Nehru's signing the pact with Liaquat Ali and he believed that the friendly policy towards Pakistan would not be successful.

During his last days, Patel began to have a negative view of the future of the Congress. He felt that the Congress has been destroyed by self-interested individuals, who serve interests of their own rather than the state. Patel was deeply upset over Nehru's way of governance. Patel remarked, "Bapu has spoilt him." Patel found himself powerless and wanted to resign from the government.

Chapter 21
A Letter

Many people held the opinion that Sardar Vallabhbhai hated Muslims and was a supporter of the Hindu organization and the *Rashtriya Swayam Sevak Sangh* (RSS). The following letter clarifies his stand as a secular Indian. A misunderstanding created a belief that the

Sardar invited them to join the Congress. However, the invitation is for rethinking and change of heart. Sardar Vallabhbhai Patel, Union Home Minister, wrote this letter to Guru Golwalkar, RSS chief, on 11 September 1948.

New Delhi,

11th Sept. 1948

Brother Sri Golwalkar,

Received your letter dated 11th August. Jawaharlal has also sent me your letter of the same date.

You are very well aware of my views on the RSS. I have expressed these thoughts at Jaipur in December last month at Lucknow in January. The people had welcomed those views. I had hoped that your people also would accept them. But they appear to have no effect on the RSS persons, nor was there any change in their programs. There

can be no doubt that the RSS did service to the Hindu Society. In the areas where there was the need for help and organisation, the young men of the RSS protected women and children and strove much for their sake. No person of understanding could have a word of objection regarding that. But the objectionable part arose when they, burning with revenge, began attacking Mussalmans. Organising Hindus and helping them is one thing but going in for revenge for its sufferings on innocent and helpless men, women and children is quite another thing.

I once again ask the RSS to join my ideals and come back to the track and help in India's development.

Yours

(SD.) Vallabhbhai Patel

Chapter 22
Patel - The Man

Wearing a toga-like dress, bald, forehead furrowed with concentration, Vallabhbhai Patel was a great person. For generations to come, a man of such a strong character as Patel, who sacrificed his entire life for the love of the country, can rarely be found. This man of simple and serious habits was made of iron. He feared none but God. He would rather break than bend down. He never broke his principles that he devotedly followed, no matter how mighty and difficult the situation was.

Though he was neither an intellectual like Nehru nor a scholar like Maulana Azad, Patel was filled with extraordinary common sense, which he used to counter and resolve multiple problems that India faced.

He is regarded as one of the greatest Indians who had the fire of Lenin and the wisdom of Bismarck. In his personal affection and devotion to Gandhi, he was second to none. His life was gentle and the elements so mixed in him that Nature might stand up and say to the world, "This was a man."

The Sardar Patel Trust

The Sardar Patel Trust was created to preserve the memory of late Shri Sardar Vallabhbhai Patel and late Shri Veer Vithalbhai Patel.

In 1975, the SP Memorial under the presidentship of Mr. Jetha Bhai V. Patel was established as the Sardar Patel Trust. Located at Karamsad, the Trust and Memorial have been founded to build qualities of leadership in a democratic polity and the spirit to serve, especially amongst the younger generations. The trust serves to maintain the ancestral house of both the brothers, award scholarships and fellowships to deserving students, establish a Women's Centre and extend help to deserving persons from economically weaker sections.

The Sardar Patel Trust is now headed by Mr. Ashok Patel, Chairman and Managing Director of GMM Pfaudler Limited and he is supported by many famous people from the industry and beyond. The trustees of the SP Trust include Dr. Amrita Patel, Chairman of National Dairy Development Board, Mr. Chiman Bhai Patel, youngest son of the great Engineer-Educationist-Politician, Dr. Bhailal Bhai D. Patel, who was closely associated with Sardar Vallabhbhai Patel, Mr. B.M. Vyas, Managing Director of Gujarat Milk Marketing Federation Ltd., (GCMMF), Mr. Bharat V. Patel, Chairman of Procter & Gamble Hygiene & Health Products Ltd., Mr. Pankaj R. Patel, Chairman and Managing Director of Zydus Cadila, one of India's leading pharmaceutical companies, Mr. Ramsinh Prabhatsinh Parmar, Chairman of Amul Dairy since October 2002 and Mr. Prayasvin Patel, who is the Managing Director of Elecon Engineering Company Limited.

On 31 October 2003, Deputy Prime Minister, Shri L.K. Advani handed over the Bharat Ratna to the Sardar Patel Trust. At a high profile function in Karamsad,

India's Deputy PM, Mr. L. K. Advani handed over the precious Bharat Ratna to Mr. Ashok Patel, President of Sardar Patel Trust, in the presence of the Chief Minister of Gujarat, Mr. Narendra Modi, Mr. Kaushik Bhai Patel, the Minister of Revenue, and Mr. Bipinbhai Patel, grandson of the late Sardar Patel. The Bharat Ratna was awarded posthumously (after death) to late Shri Sardar Patel in 1991 and was till now being looked after by his grandson Shri Bipinbhai Patel.

Additionally, few belongings of late Shri Sardar Patel, which included a charka, shawl and a tea set presented to Sardar by Lord Mountbatten, were handed over to the Sardar Patel Trust by the Chief Minister of Gujarat, Shri Narendra Modi.

Speaking on the occasion, Mr. Ashok Patel, President of Sardar Patel Trust, said, "Each October 31st, our Trust celebrates Sardar's birth anniversary. Thanks to Shri Bipin Bhai for entrusting the Trust with the Bharat Ratna, this year's celebration is of great significance to our Trust and to the people of Karamsad."

Chapter 23
Remembering Sardar Patel

Sardar Patel was a great patriot, who played a key role in rising up the national spirit of India at a time when it needed the most. He was emphatic, full of wit and wisdom, and loved Gujarat as much as he loved India and displayed immense respect for the heritage of the country.

Commemorating the great soul of India, a movie had been made which earned worldwide acclaim. The film entitled 'Sardar' is taken from 'The last days of

Sardar Patel', original film-script for Ketan Mehta's 'Sardar' by Vijay Dhondopant Tendulkar.

This biographical epic on Sardar Patel concentrates on the last five years of Sardar's life, from 1945 to 1950, when he strode on the national scene as a key figure in mixing Indian independence and uniting the nation.

This film is a tribute to the Sardar's contribution in the making of free India. This three-hour feature film is the result of the efforts of over ten years by Mr. H. M. Patel, who was a close associate of Sardar and worked in several capacities with him as Home Secretary, Cabinet Secretary, and even as his Secretary.

The *Foundation for Films on India's War of Independence* is a trust started at his behest to produce films on the subject of India's fight for independence reflecting on the contribution and role of the fighters in these movements.

The film features the well-known actor Paresh Rawal as Sardar Patel. Annu Kapoor as Mahatma Gandhi, Benjamin Gilani as Jawaharlal Nehru, Sri Vallabh Vyas as Mohammad Ali Jinnah and Tom Atler as Lord Mountbatten. The film attempts a true portrayal of the incidents as it happened. It is entertaining as well as enlightening. The movie was directed by Ketan Mehta.

On 31 October 2018, the Prime Minister of India, Narendra Modi inaugurated the statue of Sardar Patel in Gujarat. It is regarded as the world's tallest statue ranging a height of 597 ft. It serves as a token of respect for his role and leadership in the merger of the princely states and formation of the Union of India. Therefore, the statue is called the 'Statue of Unity'. It is built to commemorate the memory of such a great freedom fighter and establish him as a symbol of unity and strength.

www.ingramcontent.com/pod-product-compliance
Lightning Source LLC
LaVergne TN
LVHW091317080426
835510LV00007B/528